WHAT DOES G.T.D. STAND FOR?!?!?!
GOT THE DRAWLS!!!!!!

FIRST!!!...
I MUST
DANCE!!!!!!

DID YA MISS ME?!?!?!

HOOCHIE
BURGERS

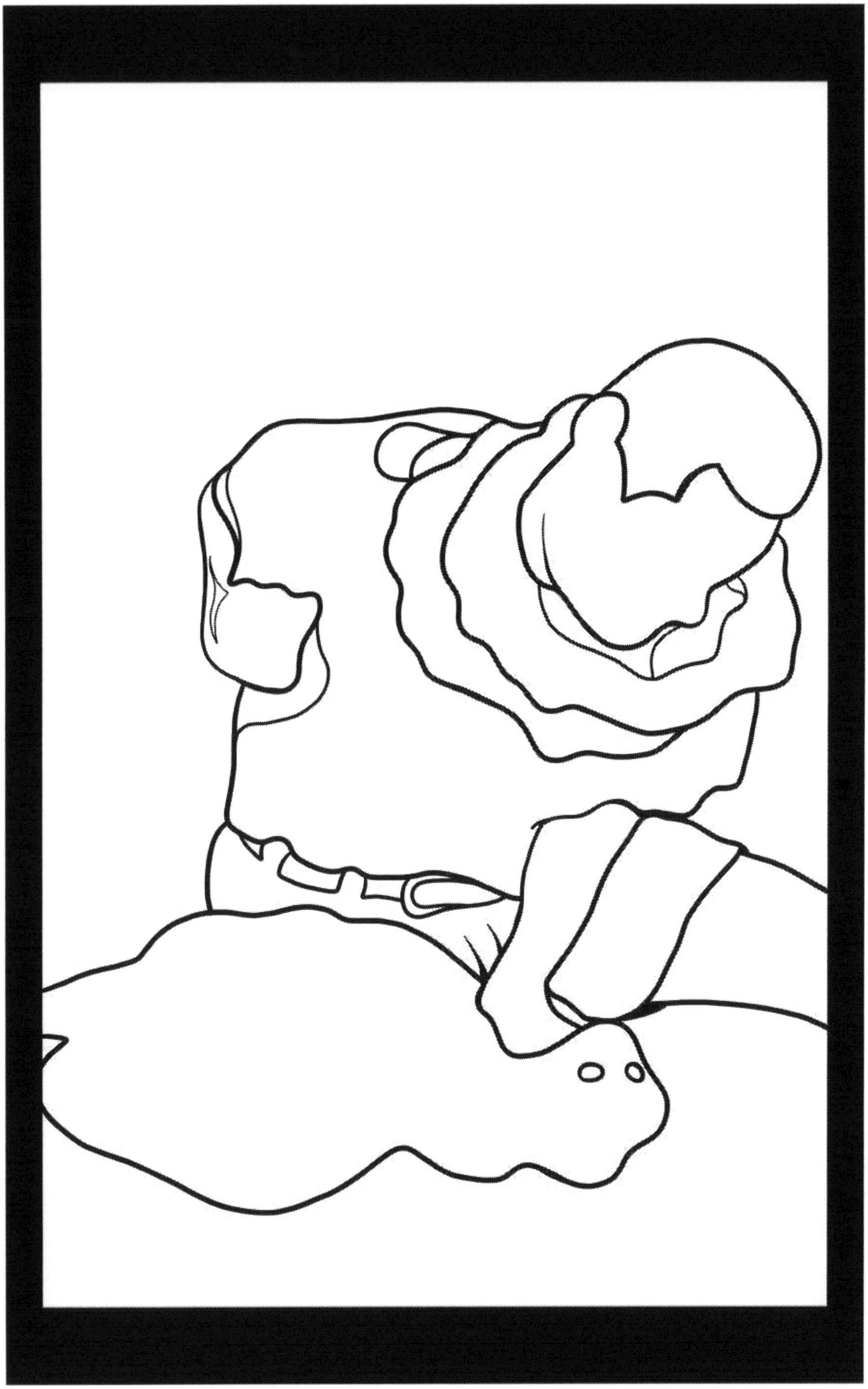

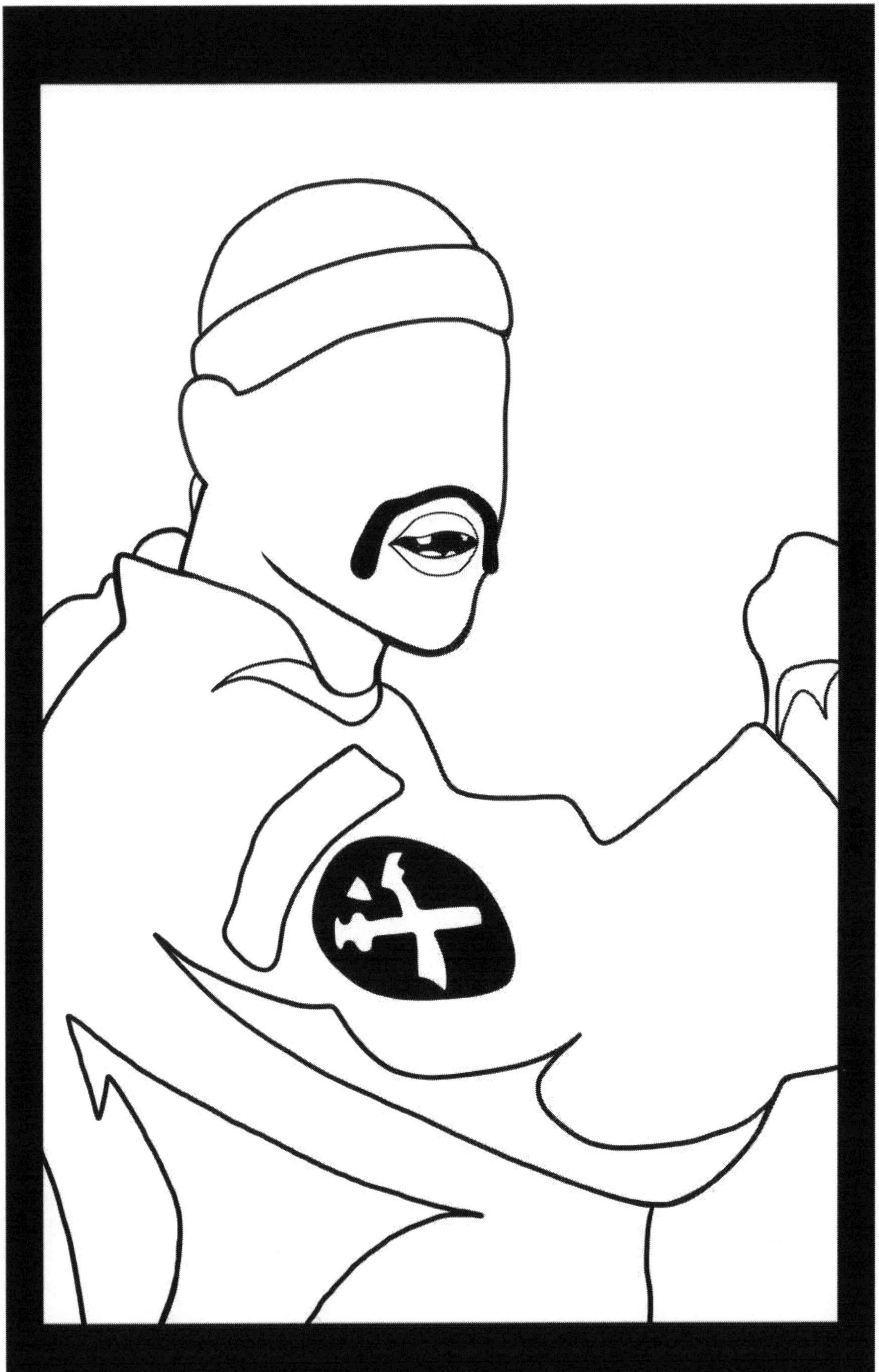

PRETTY RICKY WHAT THEY CALL EM'

SORRY I LIED TO YOU MARTIN...

Made in the USA
Middletown, DE
29 January 2022

58862812R00015